IMAGES OF ENGLAND

SHEFFIELD
SHOPS AND SHOPPING

RUTH HARMAN

TEMPUS

Frontispiece: Cole Brothers' shop at the corner of Fargate and Church Street, *c.* 1900. 'Coles Corner' was a favourite meeting place for generations of Sheffielders.

First published 2007

Tempus Publishing Limited
The Mill, Brimscombe Port,
Stroud, Gloucestershire, GL5 2QG
www.tempus-publishing.com

© Ruth Harman, 2007

The right of Ruth Harman to be identified as the Author
of this work has been asserted in accordance with the
Copyrights, Designs and Patents Act 1988.

British Library Cataloguing in Publication Data.
A catalogue record for this book is available from the British Library.

ISBN 978 0 7524 3999 0

Typesetting and origination by Tempus Publishing Limited.
Printed in Great Britain.

Contents

Acknowledgements

I extend my grateful thanks to the many people who have helped to make this book possible. Most of the photographs in it are from the extensive picture collection at Sheffield Local Studies Library – all of us who use that rich resource owe a great debt of gratitude to those who have generously given or lent photographs to the library over the years as well as to the staff who care for, catalogue and add to the collection. Thanks are also due to the Heritage Lottery Fund, which has helped to make much of it available electronically through the Picture Sheffield project and its associated website, www.picturesheffield.com. I hope that anyone who has photographs of local interest not already included in the collection will consider adding them to it for the benefit of future users.

The remaining images are from the John Lewis Partnership Archive Collection and the Marks & Spencer Company Archive, both of which kindly supplied copies, and from the collections at Sheffield Archives.

I would also like to acknowledge with thanks the following, who have generously given me permission to use privately owned and copyright images: Mr Tim Hale, John Lewis Partnership, Marks & Spencer, Rio Tinto, Sheffield City Council, Sheffield Co-operative Society Ltd and Sheffield Newspapers Ltd.

I am very grateful for help received from Fiona Maccoll, Linda Rendle, Kirsty Shields, Rebecca Walker and staff at Glasgow University Archives, and for the support and encouragement of David Buxton and Cate Ludlow at Tempus. My research for the book was mainly carried out at Sheffield Archives, in the Arts and Sports Library and in the Local Studies Library and I would like to thank my colleagues in those services for all their help. Among them I am especially grateful to Mike Spick, whose knowledge and enthusiasm, combined with unrivalled technical wizardry in the more arcane aspects of Picture Sheffield, have been invaluable.

Introduction

Whether you love it or hate it, shopping is familiar to all of us. It must be one of mankind's oldest activities - ever since people first offered things they had made, farmed, caught or found, others have been choosing those they needed or wanted. The huge increase in goods available in the nineteenth century, as Britain became a major industrial nation and expanded her global empire, together with an increasing, and increasingly wealthy, population, led to a major expansion of the retail sector. The selection of photographs in this book sets out to capture and celebrate some of its effects in one city.

The photographs mainly date from the end of the Victorian period to the mid-twentieth century and show shops and shoppers in Sheffield's city centre. For many people shopping is an important social activity, and photographs can illustrate how 'going to town' also involved dressing up, meeting friends and eating out. They show the lively variety of individual shops and wide choice of goods on offer, making some of today's streets, dominated by national chain stores, seem much less interesting by comparison. In a fiercely competitive market advertisements, sales, special offers and the display of stock to attract customers was as important as it is now. The development of the art of window dressing can be seen in several photos as the practice of cramming as much in as possible changed to presenting a few artfully arranged items to catch the attention of the passer-by. The wonderfully glamorous settings created by the Brightside and Carbrook Co-op at their City Stores deserve a special mention here. In other respects, where commerce is concerned there is often little that is really new – younger shoppers today might be surprised to learn that the whole-house furnishing packages now offered by stores like Ikea were available from T and J Roberts and Cockaynes a hundred years ago.

Since the mid-nineteenth century the pace of physical change has transformed parts of Sheffield's uniquely long, linear, shopping centre more than once and some areas, like Market Place and The Moor, have changed beyond recognition. The devastating effects of the Blitz in December 1940 and town planning schemes have played their part but relentless competition between shops and the need to expand and improve a successful business is also a factor.

Looking at photographs of the centre over a long period one can observe the endless round of musical chairs played by some shops as they moved into more prominent and prestigious sites in prosperous times or were forced into a backwater if business faltered. Sadly, all this means that Sheffield has little to offer the historian of shopfronts and there must be many who wish that at least one of the city's great Victorian department stores had survived. One of the unfortunate gaps in the record of shop interiors is the lack of pre-war photographs of palatial stores like Walshs.

Where interiors do exist they are often pristine settings devoid of people – one would love to see more of the shop assistants and their customers. Photographs showing grocery staff are one welcome exception. It is salutary to remember that shop staff worked long hours (before the black-out and other restrictions of the Second World War many shops were open in the evening) and often undertook long apprenticeships. Grocers had, for instance, to know about all the types and qualities of teas, currants and cheeses and be able to distinguish between South African and Californian tinned peaches in a blind tasting. The personal service and real knowledge of their stock that shop assistants once offered is often harder to find today.

Happily, individual shopkeepers were usually captured standing proudly in their doorway and one of the interesting features of small shops is how many were run by women. It is an aspect of their involvement in running small businesses that deserves more recognition. For mothers it was a way to combine work with domestic responsibilities and childcare, while for some widows and spinsters selling a small range of goods from their front room was a respectable way of earning a living. The story of Sheffield's many corner shops could fill another book – only a handful are included here. Similarly there are just a few photographs of shops in Sheffield's thriving suburban centres – the city has sometimes been called a collection of villages and despite pressure from supermarkets and out-of-town stores many of these local shopping centres still retain the variety of small, individual shops they had a century ago.

As nearly all the photographs date from before 1971, when Britain changed to decimal currency, the prices shown will be a mystery to anyone too young to remember the shillings and old pennies of £, s and d. For their benefit – there were twenty shillings in a pound, so one shilling equals five pence. There were twelve pennies in a shilling – so sixpence is two and a half pence. Because of inflation and changes in relative wealth, trying to indicate the real modern equivalent of prices in the past is actually much more difficult and complicated than one might expect. For anyone who wishes to pursue this there are two very helpful websites that will calculate the current value of money from past years – www.measuringworth.com and www.ex.ac.uk/~RDavies/arian/current/howmuch.html .

Meanwhile, to forget all the recent changes that have brought us out-of-town supermarkets and retail parks, Meadowhall and internet shopping, just turn the page and indulge in some nostalgic armchair shopping in a Sheffield of the past.

one

New Streets,
New Shops…

In the nineteenth century the centre of Sheffield was transformed from that of a historic market town to one worthy of a Victorian city. In 1875 the town council began a programme of improvements that went on for over thirty years as existing streets were widened and new ones created, providing opportunities for rebuilding on a grander scale. Older properties such as these shops in Snig Hill, photographed in around 1890, were bought up and demolished. The building on the right with its open shop front and jettied upper stories, typical of timber-framed buildings, was probably Tudor or even medieval in date.

Market Place and the top of Angel Street with Montague Burton's impressive new shop, c. 1933. Its neighbours were built between 1890 and 1910, most to designs by local architects. They replaced older properties of two to three storeys dating from the eighteenth and early nineteenth centuries.

A view from the top of High Street looking down to Market Place, *c.* 1895. High Street had long been one of the main shopping streets in the town, linking the markets with the area around the parish church, Cutlers' Hall and old Town Hall at Church Gates. After lengthy negotiations over property rights, all these older buildings on the south side were demolished so the street could be widened by more than twenty feet in 1896. Foster's the drapers was one of the shops that was rebuilt in the same position, but on the new building line.

This view was taken some fifteen to twenty years later. On the right is part of Foster's splendid new shop, faced in stone, with towers and turrets in a baronial style. It was the first shop in Sheffield to have an elevator. The very large block a few doors down is Walsh's. By now the bus services were supplemented with electric trams running across the city, making it easier for people to travel in from the suburbs to shop.

Fargate was widened in 1879, allowing everything on the west side, between Coles' shop at the bottom corner and the Georgian properties seen here near the top, to be rebuilt. The new frontages were designed in a variety of styles incorporating Classical, Gothic and Renaissance details, which were more easily appreciated before they became blackened by the city's sooty atmosphere. Shops like Hartley Brothers the tailors took the opportunity of redevelopment on Pinstone Street nearby to move to a modern shop in a prestigious position.

The lower end of Pinstone Street, c. 1930. The street was transformed from a narrow lane about 1890 and was soon lined with smart shops with offices and flats above. By the 1930s the city centre had lost most of its residents to the new suburban housing estates and many upper floors were unused until the recent revival of urban apartment living. Sheffield has never had grand arcades like those in Leeds – apart from the one through Cockaynes (see page 64), there was only the small Cambridge arcade, the entrance is visible between Richards' drapery shop and Barney Goodman the tailor.

The Moor (known as South Street until 1922) in about 1925. Pinstone Street linked the older shopping area around the markets and High Street with this long, gently sloping street at the southern end of Sheffield's uniquely linear shopping centre. The Moor was developed in the nineteenth century and Earl Fitzwilliam made a short-lived attempt to exercise his rival market rights for Ecclesall Manor by opening the Ecclesall Bazaar here in 1829. It closed in 1850. By the 1920s the street was lined with shops (many duplicating those at the other end of the centre) as well as banks, pubs, chapels and cinemas. Both of the new shops on the right are fronted in faience, the glazed 'self-cleaning' terracotta fashionable in the early twentieth century. Available in white, pastel green and yellow, with a wide choice of decorative mouldings, it was popular as a defence against Sheffield's smoky air.

The Moor in 1953, with Atkinson's site on the left (see pages 97 and 100). Although the gaps left by damage in the Blitz of 1940 are very evident, far more survived than is now generally realised. The remaining buildings were demolished for the complete redevelopment of The Moor as part of the plans for post-war improvements. The Trebor's lorry was a welcome sight as sweets finally came off ration in February. In 1942, when sweet rationing started, the weekly allowance was restricted to three ounces per person.

Temporary shops at the bottom of The Moor, near the junction with Young Street, still in use in 1965. They were typical of the single-storey units allowed under wartime building restrictions to replace bomb-damaged properties. The site is now occupied by the government offices at Moorfoot. The Sheffield and Ecclesall Co-op on Ecclesall Road can be seen in the background.

By the mid-1960s the redevelopment of The Moor was complete. Although the trams had gone and the new buildings lacked the lively variety of their pre-war predecessors the street was still a major shopping attraction. There were three large department stores – Atkinsons, Roberts Brothers and Debenhams – as well as a Marks & Spencer, British Home Stores and Woolworths. The biggest change to come was pedestrianisation in 1978, following the successful removal of traffic from Fargate in 1971.

two

Markets and Street Traders

Sheffield's markets have been an important part of local shopping provision for centuries, supplying people with a wide range of goods long before shops as we know them existed. In 1296 Edward II granted a charter to Thomas de Furnival, Lord of the Manor of Sheffield, giving him the right to hold a weekly market in the town on Tuesdays. This right descended to the Dukes of Norfolk and remained with them until 1899 when the 15th duke sold the markets to the Corporation for £526,000 (over £200 million at today's values). The lucrative right to levy tolls on incoming goods and receive the rents from market stalls justified the dukes' considerable expenditure on new market buildings in the eighteenth and nineteenth centuries.

The Norfolk Market was the first general covered market hall, built on the site of the Tontine Inn, near the Shambles and the Corn Exchange. It was designed by the local architects J.G. Weightman and M.E. Hadfield in an imposing Tuscan style and built of brick with stone dressings. It opened on Christmas Eve 1851. The building was altered by the city council in 1924 and was eventually demolished in 1959.

A sweet stall in the Norfolk Market Hall decorated in celebration of the royal wedding of the Duke of York (later George V) and Mary, daughter of the Duke of Teck, in July 1893.

An impression of the interior from the 1862 *Illustrated Guide to Sheffield*. The hall was 296 feet long by 115 feet wide, with an iron-framed glass roof and additional lighting from lunettes above the stalls that occupied the space around the walls. Two double rows of stalls ran down the centre, with a gap for the cross-avenue running between the side entrances in Dixon Lane and Castle Folds. This marked the division between the fruit and vegetable stalls at the Haymarket end and those selling fancy goods, small wares, hosiery, shoes and hardware at the Corn Exchange end. A large Italianate stone fountain stood in the centre of the hall.

Above: Marks & Spencer originated with a stall set up in Leeds market in 1884 by Michael Marks, a Jewish refugee from Poland. All the goods for sale cost a penny, equivalent to about thirty pence at today's prices. He went into partnership with Tom Spencer in 1894 and the business flourished, having thirty-six outlets by 1900. The first one in Sheffield was their stall in the centre of the Norfolk Market Hall, set up some four years before this photo was taken in 1901.

Right: The entry for the Norfolk Market in White's *Sheffield Directory* for 1900 includes Marks & Spencer and shows the wide range of goods available.

NORFOLK MARKET HALL.
(*Haymarket.*)

1 Burgon & Co. confectioners
2 Heathcote John William, grocer

3, 4, 5, 25, 27 & 28 Rodgers Thos. Parkin, music seller
6 Jackson Bros. leather merchants
7 & 8 Glossop Thos. cutlery manufr
9 Tatton Adam, ironmonger
10, 12 & 41 Slack Robert, manufacturing confectioner
11 Melbourne Miss Mary Ann, glass & china dealer
13, 18 & 19 Southern William Geo. cutler
14 Cocker Arthur Pearson, hosier
15-16 Schofield J. & Sons, boot mas
17 Darbyshire Edwd. cutlery dealer
18 & 19 Southern Wm. Geo. cutler
20 Nichol John, hosier
21 Peat John, biscuit dealer
22 Nuttall Thos. sewing machine dlr
23 Jarvis James, hosier & smallware dealer
24 SUPERINTENDENT'S OFFICE; Jos. Matthews, superintendent
25, 3, 4, 5, 27 & 28 Rodgers Thomas P. musical instrument seller
26 Rodgers & Pilkington, booksellers
27, 3, 4, 5, 25 & 28 Rodgers Thomas P. musical instrument seller
29 Walkland Frederick, glass & china dealer
30 Cousins John Albert, phrenologst
31 & 32 Hindley Joseph B. tool dlr
34 Smith Mrs. Ann. basket maker

35 Priestley Henry, refreshment rms
36 Cheetham Thomas, ironmonger
37 Crosland Brothers, nurserymen
38 Cope Mrs. Ada, cordial manufr
39, 40, 42 & 44 Smith Noah, basket maker & leather goods
41, 10 & 12 Slack Robert, manufacturing confectioner
43 Wattam Thomas, cutlery manufr
45 Fleming John & Sons, hair dressers &c
46 Warde Thomas, secondhand bookseller
47-48 Denniff Francis Wm. fruiterer
.... *Centre of Hall* ....
Hirst Mrs. Sarah Ann, fruiterer
Simonite Frank, florist
Conyers John, florist
Artindale Wm. & Son, florists &c
Barker Tom J. florist
Robinson William Hy. fruiterer
Cook Henry, nurseryman
Nation Walter G. nurseryman
Woodfield James, nurseryman
Seagrave Samuel W. seedsman
McGrail Mrs. Mary, greengrocer
Howarth John, india rubber stamp maker
Howarth Mrs. Annie, John & Co. smallware dealers
Marks & Spencer, smallware dlrs
Howarth A. & J. & Co. smallware dealers
Skellington George Herbert, smallware dealer
Davison Bernard, cap manufactr
Charlesworth John, draper
Wainwright Harry, herring curer
Popple Geo. W. joiners' tool mfr

Fitzalan Chambers, Haymarket, *c*. 1916. These were at the lower end of the Fitzalan Market, which extended down the hill from Market Place and was built as the Shambles in 1784. When it was remodelled in 1855-56 it included a wine vault used for many years by Sheffield wine and spirit merchants Duncan Gilmour and Co. They had a national reputation as whisky blenders but also found fame among teetotallers for their non-alcoholic Hop Bitter Beer. At this date the offices upstairs were used for commercial business training by the De Bear Schools.

The Killing Shambles were slaughterhouses occupying an unsavoury range of buildings beside the river Don between Lady's Bridge and Blonk Bridge, where Castlegate is now. The meat was sold in the markets and the city's butchers' shops. The Shambles were demolished after the new city abattoir opened in 1929, but this end block survived in use as a shop for several years.

The open–air Sheaf Market, popularly known as the Rag n'Tag, *c.* 1930. It was a complete contrast to the more orderly grandeur of the Norfolk Market Hall, and its irregular lanes and alleys and collection of ramshackle buildings and pitches housed a bewildering variety of goods. This view was taken from the bottom of Commercial Street, looking across the market to the larger sheds of Castlefolds Market on Broad Street.

The entrance on Broad Street, *c.* 1930. The reason for the bunting is not clear but the bright lights over the entrance brightened up the rather dreary surroundings.

Above: Sheaf Market, *c.* 1963, looking towards the newly completed Park Hill flats on the right with the even bigger Hyde Park complex rising on the left. The markets were within easy walking distance of the thousands of people who lived in the Park area. Ogley's pet shop had recently set up business in the market in more substantial premises than most traders had.

Below: Crowds thronging Sheaf Market in 1967. Although it was shabby and run down, the market was still very popular. It was eventually closed on 3 March 1973 and the new indoor Sheaf Market opened the following week.

'Potty' Edwards, one of the best-known characters in the old Sheaf Market, entertaining the crowds at his china stall in 1973.

The bottom of Broad Street in 1957 with Castlefolds Market, the city's wholesale fruit and vegetable market, on the right. In its unprepossessing wooden and corrugated iron sheds everything from sacks of potatoes to pineapples and other exotic fruits packed in wooden crates was available to local greengrocers and stallholders. Although most traders had vans or lorries, a few still used horse-drawn carts. After the new wholesale markets at Acres Hill opened in 1961, Castlefolds closed and the indoor Sheaf Market was later built on the site.

The interior of the newly opened Sheaf Market in 1973. Its bright lights and long rows of uniform, numbered stalls lacked the atmosphere of its predecessor but it was well used for twenty-five years.

Shoppers at Hallam's stall in Sheaf Market, 1993. The main food market was Castle Market nearby, which had stalls designed for the sale of meat and fish.

The Sheaf Market also had a good reputation for household goods such as curtain and dress materials, haberdashery and fabric remnants. It closed in the late 1990s for redevelopment, some of its traders transferring to stalls in Castle Market. The building was demolished in 2002.

Left: Street sellers or hawkers were often among the poorest class of market traders – they did not need to rent a stall if they sold goods from a barrow or cart, although they did need a licence. Like these two traders selling vegetables in Sheaf Street in around 1900, country people could bring their own produce into town in the way they had for hundreds of years.

Below: A gaily decorated ice-cream kiosk outside the Punch Bowl Inn on The Moor in 1901. An ice cream was a popular treat for children and shoppers so vendors pitched their stalls and carts, and later vans, in busy streets and at the markets (see page 22). Some of the Italian immigrants in the late nineteenth century were skilled ice-cream makers and set up successful businesses. Luigi Granelli and his family came to Sheffield about 1900 and his brother, five nephews and a niece are among the ten ice-cream sellers listed as his employees in the 1901 census. Note that the passing boy is wearing clogs.

three

The Butcher,
the Baker…

CAFE

TUCKWOODS
RELIABLE QUALITY

THE FAMOUS
"SUNNY CUP"
TEA.

Tuckwood's grocery store in Fargate, looking towards the street entrance, *c.* 1930. The firm had its own bakery and factory, making bread, cakes, confectionery and jams. Like all high-class grocers and provision merchants, Tuckwood's blended their own teas, serving 'Sunnycup' in their café. Although by this time many goods were pre-packaged, most grocers also sold things like teas, dried fruit and spices loose, weighed out by overall-clad shop assistants like those on the left, and presented to the customer in paper bags.

The view from the front towards the entrance to the café at the rear of the long, narrow shop. The luxurious café included both a ladies' boudoir and a gentlemen's smoking room.

On the other side of Fargate, Arthur Davy's grocers shop and café opened in 1882 in a building (now occupied by W H Smith) decorated with the carved heads of a pig and ox to represent the hams, sausages, potted meats and pork pies sold. The manager in the 1920s was John Arthy, seen here dressed formally in wing collar, bow tie and spats. The café menu displayed on the wall would have included the range of coffees roasted in the shop – although Davy's closed in 1972, older Sheffielders speak nostalgically of the delicious aroma that wafted down Fargate!

Although many shops on The Moor were destroyed in the Blitz, others survived, only to be demolished when the street was redeveloped in the 1950s and '60s. Davy's had occupied this building on the corner of Bennett Lane since before 1900 and was one of the few businesses still trading in their pre-war premises in 1952.

Ferdinand Gebhardt was one of Sheffield's nineteenth-century German immigrants. By 1891 there were 298 Germans living in the town and while some were connected with the steel industry or were teachers, clerks or musicians, there were several who set up pork butchers' shops. Gebhardt's first shop was on The Moor – this branch in Pond Street was photographed in 1894. The largest immigrant community in the town at this date were the Irish, who had less influence on eating habits than later arrivals. In the twentieth century, immigrants from Bangladesh, China, India and Pakistan set up shops selling foodstuffs imported from their homelands and introduced a wide variety of new foods to Sheffield.

Alfred Oliver at the doorway of his and his brother's shop on Staniforth Road, *c.* 1930. While some of the English meat was likely to be from the new city abattoir, refrigeration enabled butchers to buy from wholesalers getting meat from other parts of the country as well as from South America and New Zealand.

Above: Henry Lawson White's grocers shop in London Road, *c.* 1900. John Arthy (1876-1976), later the manager of Davy's shop on Fargate (see page 29), is the third assistant from the left. Although the prominent advertisement for cheese bought directly from the farmers would have helped to reassure customers that the foods were fresh, there were no hygiene restrictions to prevent them being displayed on the street.

Right: An eye-catching display at Crookes in the early 1900s. The chickens have been plucked but would have been sold with their heads and feet on so customers could use the neck and feet as well as the giblets to make stock for soups or gravy.

Smartly dressed staff outside Lipton's branch at Attercliffe in 1914. Lipton's were grocers and butchers, and their teas, which were widely available, made them a household name. Thomas Lipton founded the firm in Glasgow in 1871. He had a flair for using advertising and publicity, and rapidly expanded the business across Scotland. In the 1880s shops were opened throughout England and Wales, establishing one of the earliest national networks of retail branches. The sugar at 3lbs for 2d to 'overweight buyers' is not actually a special offer to fat customers, but an inducement to buy a greater weight than the usual quantity of one or two pounds.

Opposite above: The interior with its cool and hygienic, marble-topped and tiled counter. Attractive packaging and special offers were an important part of the firm's competitive marketing. Canned foods, first introduced in the mid-1800s, were now widespread and made exotic and out-of-season produce available all year. Other foods, which might be locally produced, were still wrapped traditionally, such as butter in muslin.

Opposite below: The Shiregreen branch of the B & C Co-op in Bellhouse Road in 1921. The Co-op offered as comprehensive a range of goods as possible so that members could do all their shopping at their shops. They often sold different types of food together when other local shops were more specialised, and so can be seen as forerunners of the modern supermarket. Here they displayed fruit and vegetables in the left-hand window while the right side had a traditional open counter for fish and poultry.

The Maypole Dairy Co. was a national company originally dealing in butter. By 1921 they had seventeen branches in the city – this is the Tinsley branch photographed at about that time. Unlike Lipton's it seems that the shop's staff were all men.

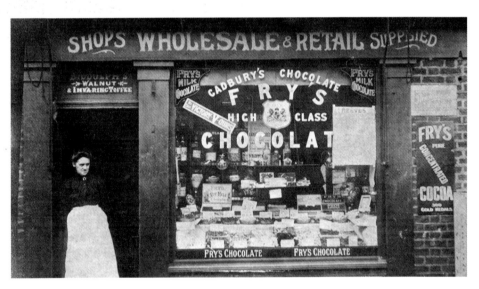

This unidentified sweet shop would have delighted chocolate lovers around 1900. Introduced to Europe from Mexico in the sixteenth century, for a long time chocolate was only available as a luxury beverage. High import duties on cocoa beans were eventually reduced and after Fry's of Bristol developed a process of mixing chocolate, sugar and cocoa butter to make bars of eating chocolate in 1850 it became very popular. Milk chocolate was invented in Switzerland in 1876. Fry's and their main rivals, Cadbury's of Bournville and Rowntree's of York, were leading Quaker families. They all supported teetotalism and cocoa was often promoted as an alternative to beer. The 'Invaring' in the 'Walnut and Invaring Toffee' is a mystery.

The family grocery business founded by Joseph Pollard had this shop on the corner of Glossop Road and Fitzwilliam Street from around 1880 until it closed in 1979. The interior, seen here in 1974, was then a much-loved treasure trove of speciality teas and coffees, jams and preserves, cheeses and exotic delicacies that were hard to find elsewhere in the city.

Mrs E.T. Page and her son at her shop on the corner of Hill Street and John Street, Highfield, c. 1898. In working-class residential areas there was a shop on almost every corner. Many were run by women who were able to combine childcare and their domestic duties with work that helped support them and their families. Farms on the outskirts of the city, at Meersbrook and Manor, were only a mile or two away and so would have been able to deliver fresh milk after the morning and evening milking each day. Customers could take along a jug to be filled from a wooden churn.

A patient and cheerful queue outside a butcher's shop at Crookes in the First World War. Throughout the conflict the German navy tried to cut off imported supplies of food and other goods to Britain and their U-boat submarines were a deadly threat to the merchant navy. By 1917 over 300,000 tons of shipping a month were being lost and later that year panic buying led to shortages. The Ministry of Food introduced rationing in January 1918, first of sugar and then of meat, in order to control supplies rather than to reduce consumption.

Local shops in Netherthorpe Place, Port Mahon, in 1939. When people had little space and few facilities for storing fresh food at home a daily trip to the butcher, baker and greengrocer was normal. Family firms like Herbert Savage, the butcher, or Hancock's the baker a few doors up the street, often had shops in more than one suburban shopping area.

The Blitz in December 1940 caused widespread disruption to every aspect of life throughout the city. Emergency planning ensured that essential supplies, such as bread, were maintained and in local shops like this one staff reopened despite the damage. Although bread was not rationed during the war consumption was restricted for a short time in 1948.

The grocery department at the B & C's Attercliffe branch on Attercliffe Road in 1962. The Co-op was especially strong in this working-class area and provided for almost every need from the cradle to the grave. Other departments in adjacent and nearby shops included a chemist's, tailoring, footwear, furnishing, wallpaper, painting and decorating and a funeral director.

The interior of the Attercliffe branch in 1962, with items arranged on the counter and shelves in the traditional way. The prices and brand names have changed but the shop does not look very different from Lipton's nearly half a century earlier (see page 33).

The grocery department at the Brightside and Carbrook Co-op at Margetson Crescent, Parson Cross, when it opened in 1951. It was the last counter-service store to be opened. In future, new stores would be self-service and older stores were gradually converted. The metal shelf at the front of the counter was handy for customers to rest their shopping bags on.

Mr J.R. Harper, the president of the Society, serving one of the first customers at the opening. The man on the right, wearing the grocer's traditional white overall, is probably Mr Chapman, the manager of the store.

An eager crowd gathered outside the new self-service store at Northern Avenue, on the Arbourthorne housing estate, when it was opened in 1958. Local shops were especially important when few families had a car and taking a pram on a bus to the city centre was impossible.

The Richmond Park Road Co-op at Handsworth in 1959, newly arranged for self-service. The opportunity to browse and choose food and other goods for oneself revolutionised grocery shopping in the 1950s. Traditional counter-service in some bakers, butchers and greengrocers still continues, though the number of shops has been dramatically reduced as many people buy everything they need at supermarkets.

four

Hearth and
Home

The deserted household linens department at G.H. Crossley's drapers, on the corner of Angel Street and Castle Street, in 1940 (see also pages 56 and 57). Staff and customers were almost invariably banished when formal record photographs of shop interiors were taken, presumably for fear that they would distract attention from the carefully arranged displays and make the place look untidy.

The interior of the drapery department at the Brightside and Carbrook Co-op, Page Hall Road, Firth Park, in 1964, the year before it closed. The shelves behind the counter were originally designed to hold bolts of cloth like those on the top shelves on the right, rather than the sheets, blankets and eiderdowns lower down. Although there was less demand for fabrics as more people bought their clothes ready-made, the shop still stocked a wide range of buttons, trimmings and other haberdashery items for home sewing, displayed on the counter and stands.

Right: Charles George's traditional chemists and druggists shop at 70 Fargate, on the corner of Leopold Street, in about 1900. Chemists prepared their products from chemicals, while druggists used plants. Their extensive knowledge equipped them to make a wide variety of products such as sauces, paints and dyes as well as medicines. The distinctively-shaped glass bottles or carboys, filled with coloured water and displayed prominently in the windows, were a typical sign of chemist's shops by this date.

Below: James Furnival Eardley was one of the new breed of registered pharmaceutical chemists, regulated by legislation passed in 1868. By 1902 he had four family chemists shops on the west side of Sheffield, including this one at Broomhill, as well as a mineral water factory near Ecclesall Road. The large lamp above the doorway would have been a reassuring sign for anyone who needed medicine urgently at night.

Boots' new shop at the junction of High Street with Fargate, *c.* 1900. The first branch in Sheffield was in Snig Hill, but this became the main shop when it opened here in 1897. By 1901 there were seventeen other branches in the city. The firm was developed by Jesse Boot, whose father had a shop selling herbal remedies in Nottingham. From selling cut-price patent medicines in the 1870s Boot built up the largest chemist's shop business in the country with 181 branches by 1900 and 560 by 1914. He extended the range of goods sold to include stationery and fancy goods and for many years his shops had successful and popular libraries lending light fiction.

Opposite above: George Eastman invented the Kodak camera in the USA in 1888 and many Sheffield chemists expanded their businesses into the new popular market for photography from the 1890s (see also page 111). Joseph Jackson opened this shop on Abbeydale Road about 1898 and devoted nearly half the window and shop space to cameras and photographic equipment.

Opposite below: The interior of the shop, however, was still dominated by the traditional chemist's counter with a high screen hiding the dispensary where powders, pills, ointments and medicines were measured, mixed and packaged. The tall shelves held rows of labelled jars and bottles containing drugs and chemicals in the form of liquids, powders or creams. Rows of drawers lower down were often used for storing herbs and roots.

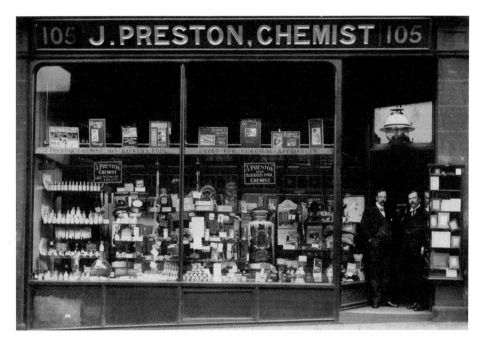

Job Preston's business was established in High Street before moving to Fargate in 1894 and then to this shop in Barker's Pool in 1903, when this photo was probably taken. Preston's were not only chemists and druggists, with prescription books dating back to 1823, but were also specialist suppliers of scientific and laboratory equipment. Their services were important to the research departments of many of Sheffield's steel firms whose discoveries enhanced the city's worldwide reputation for metallurgy.

Preston's moved from Barker's Pool to West Street in 1926 when the shop was bought for redevelopment. The shops of all the neighbouring businesses such as Samuel Barnsley, carver and gilder, and Foster's art shop were also demolished and the Regent Cinema (later the Gaumont) opened on the site on Boxing Day 1927.

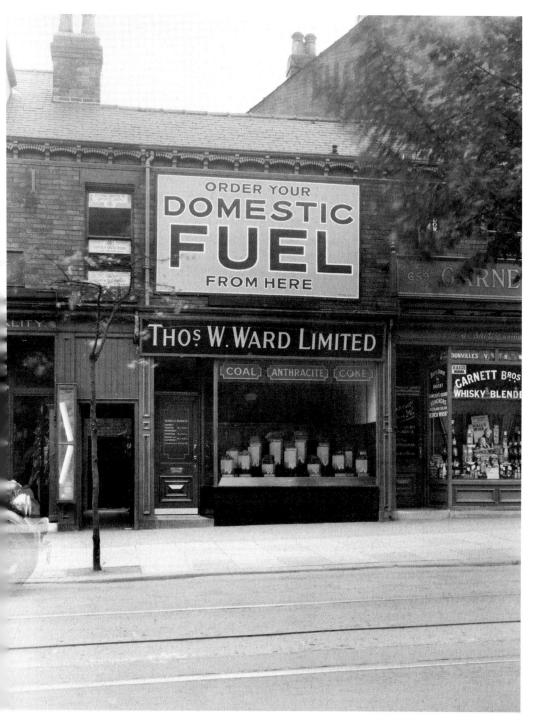

Tommy Ward's of Savile Street were best known as factors to Sheffield's industries, supplying coal, metal and machinery to many of the steel works, but also had several suburban coal offices for the sale of domestic fuel. This artfully presented display of different types of coal for household fires, cooking stoves and hot water boilers enticed shoppers at Hunter's Bar in 1937.

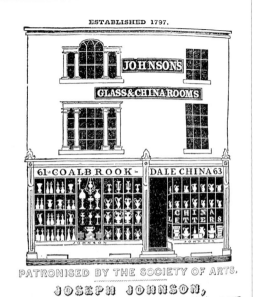

An advertisement for Joseph Johnson's china shop from Rodger's *Sheffield Trade Directory* 1841. By then Fargate was well-established as one of the town's principal shopping streets and Johnson's large shop front extended the full width of the elegant two-bay building. The large windows with their small panes typical of early nineteenth-century shop fronts show a fine display of decanters, vases and jugs. By 1841 improved transport by canal and railway made a much wider range of goods, such as Coalbrookdale china, more easily available. The water filters Johnson manufactured were increasingly necessary as the town grew and people depended on a common water supply of often dubious quality. As awareness of the danger of water-borne disease grew, especially after the cholera epidemic of 1832, filtering water for domestic use was seen as an easy way of improving one's personal supply. Many Georgian shops such as this one were swept away in the widening of Fargate at the end of the century.

Charles Constantine's ironmongers shop at the top end of Fargate (now Barker's Pool), *c.* 1905. The business was founded in 1831 and stocked household furniture as well as builders' and general ironmongery. It moved to Carver Street in 1910 when the row of shops next to Wilson Peck's was bought as the site of Cinema House, which opened three years later.

Most suburban shopping centres had at least one furniture shop. James Oldham's business on the corner of Netherthorpe Place and St Philip's Road (pictured *c.* 1935) had been established in the area for over thirty years. It helpfully offered credit to customers who could not afford to pay for items all at once. Note the Belisha beacon. These flashing amber globes on black and white poles indicated points where pedestrians could cross roads more safely. They were named after the Minister of Transport, Leslie Hoare-Belisha, who introduced them in 1934.

By the early 1930s the Sheffield Furnishing Co., at London Road, Highfield, had replaced the traditional horse and cart with this small fleet of delivery lorries supplied by the Deighton Motor Co.

Charles Smith and Sons Ltd were general tinplate workers and hardware merchants, selling their goods on the corner of Norfolk Street and Arundel Street. In 1910 the shop still retained the large windows with small panes of crown glass typical of late eighteenth-century shops. The slight curve in each pane resulted from the glass-blowing process, giving them the uneven appearance visible here. The doorway below the fine display of watering cans and baskets seems completely obstructed with goods. Gable-end walls were ideal sites for theatre posters.

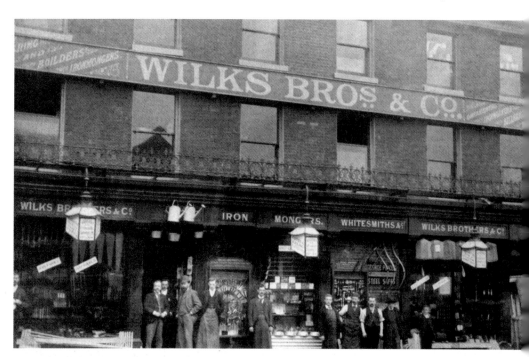

Wilks' ironmongers shop at Furnival Gate, c. 1890. They were a long-established family business, selling everything from household ironmongery and builders' tools to ploughs and other farm implements. They also made a wide range of plain and decorative wrought iron gates and railings like the balustrade above the shop's fascia.

Right: The firm moved to High Street in 1922, but only stayed for four years before transferring to Exchange Street. Although window-shoppers enjoyed the hardware on offer, prime sites like this were much sought after by fashion and other high value retailers and Saxone Shoes soon moved in (see page 59).

Below: A glass-roofed rear extension to the shop in High Street for kitchenware and other household goods such as the mangle. As the stacks of frying pans and buckets show, there was little attempt to display such essential items artistically and this sort of arrangement enabled large quantities of stock to be carried in a limited space. In the 1920s kettles and saucepans in the newly available shiny aluminium were as appealing as stainless steel is today. Being lightweight and rust-free it seemed far superior to traditional heavy cast-iron pans, and even to enamelware, which could get chipped and stained.

Above: More buckets on display in Langsett Road. As there is only a temporary sign this photo was probably taken just after Mr Lingard set up his own business about 1905, and he must be the modestly proprietorial figure in the doorway of his new shop. On the right are washtubs, a washboard for rubbing clothes and a washing dolly, which had wooden prongs at the bottom, for swirling clothes around in the tub. Unfortunately the elbow grease needed for using these utensils couldn't be bought!

Left: In 1921 Lingard moved to an adjacent shop, where the business carried on for many years. Although this photo dates from the 1920s many of the items on display, like the rolls of chicken wire, galvanised metal buckets and different sizes of spade, can still be bought in traditional ironmonger's today.

five

Fashion

Above: Robert Hanbidge's second shop on Fargate, *c.* 1905. His successful business as a high-class hatter, hosier, shirt maker, glover and general outfitter already occupied large premises on the other corner of Fargate and Norfolk Row when he expanded into this new shop unit. The imposing building was completed in 1892 for the Young Men's Christian Association, who occupied the upper floors.

Left: A design for part of Hanbidge's shop front with decorative surrounds to the large windows that were possible after the invention of machine-produced plate glass in the nineteenth century. Redevelopment and fierce competition among High Street retailers to have the most up-to-date shop fronts, signs and fittings, result in constant change and renewal and so the survival of shops in their original state is very rare.

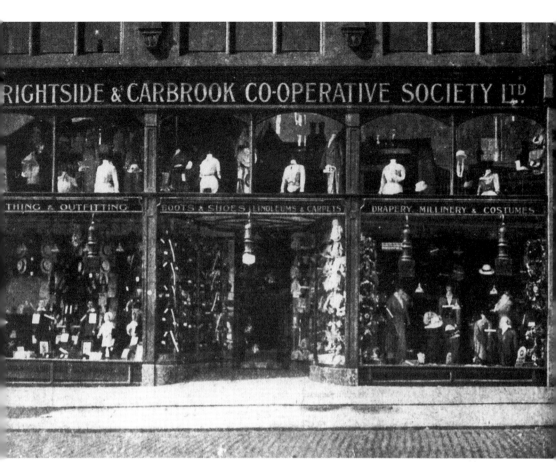

The Brightside and Carbrook Co-op's branch at Page Hall Road, Firth Park in 1914. The shop's range of clothes rivalled those of the city-centre drapers. The upper tier of large windows, known as 'entresol lunettes' were a development in shop-front design that can be seen in other photos. They helped to light the first-floor showrooms and allowed passengers on the upper decks of passing buses and trams to window shop.

Above: This handsome block with its crow-stepped gable and tall chimneys was built in 1894 on the corner of Angel Street and Castle Street for G.H. Hovey. Their previous department store on the site burnt down the year before, when it was barely ten years old. By 1914 the building was occupied by Briggs' shoe shop and the drapers G.H. Crossley, who later expanded to occupy the whole of the Angel Street frontage and some of the upper floor space (see page 42 and opposite).

Opposite above: The ladieswear department in G.H. Crossley's shop in Angel Street in 1940 (see also page 42 and opposite). The building was destroyed by bombing in December that year. Like many other goods, clothing was rationed during the war and a system of coupons was in operation from 1940 to March 1949.

Opposite below: The shop of Colver and Co. in the former post office at Market Place in April 1930, shortly before they moved round the corner into King Street. They were one of Sheffield's oldest firms of hatters, glovers, hosiers, outfitters and tailors, originally established by William Colver in Angel Street in the 1860s. The Fitzalan Market building was demolished soon after this photo was taken and Burton's shop was built on this end of the site (see page 62).

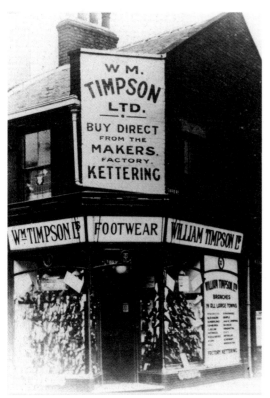

Left: A small branch of Timpson's at London Road, Highfield, *c.* 1925. William Timpson opened his first shoe shop in Manchester in 1865 and later set up a boot factory in his home town of Kettering to supply his growing chain of shops. He laid great emphasis on good customer service and striking window displays.

Below: Timpson's shop in Pinstone Street in 1952. It had occupied this prime site opposite the Town Hall since 1924. Due to post-war building restrictions the shop still had its stylish 1930s signage of large, separately applied illuminated letters on a black vitrolite fascia. After petrol rationing ended in May 1950, increasing traffic made the provision of crossings for pedestrians even more important. In addition to the Belisha beacons, black and white 'zebra' stripes on the road surface were introduced in that year to make them more obvious to motorists.

Above: Saxone Shoes were established in Market Place from about 1910 and moved to High Street in 1927. Only their smart signage survived the Blitz in December 1940. They returned to a new shop on the same site in 1956.

Right: Although this shoe shop at Woodhouse was small its proprietors used its large fascia (which would probably fall foul of today's advertising regulations) to maximum effect. They obviously didn't worry about shoplifting either – disregarding the modern shoe seller's convention of putting only one shoe from a pair on display.

Ormrod and Faulkner's shop on Haymarket garlanded for a royal visit, probably that of King Edward VII and Queen Alexandra in July 1905. Many shops put out very elaborate decorations for royal visits, rivalling the flags, banners and festoons in the streets (see page 97). The upper floors of shop premises were often used as offices by accountants, insurance agents and similar professions – on this occasion the exciting opportunity to get a good view of the royal procession would have outweighed the impropriety of climbing out of the window.

Charles Henry Cleathero in the doorway of his tailor's shop in Waingate, a short distance from Ormrod and Faulkner, c. 1902. People who set up their own businesses quite often announced the name of their previous employer as a sort of testimonial to their own quality (see also page 52). The slightly projecting wooden shop front with decorative carving is a fine example of its kind.

George Binns' shop at the top of The Moor soon after it opened in 1889. Its impressive front disguised its curious shape, dictated by the narrow triangular site bounded by Carver Street on the left and Button Lane behind. The business offered a wide range of clothing and accessories for men and boys as well as a traditional tailoring service.

Burton's the tailors splendid new Art Deco shop on Market Place and High Street, c. 1933. Montague Burton, a Jewish immigrant from Lithuania, started in business in Chesterfield, but later moved to Leeds. He revolutionised men's tailoring, being the first to produce made-to-measure suits and coats at prices working men could afford. By 1930, he had factories making both cloth and clothing in order to supply a nationwide chain of over 400 shops.

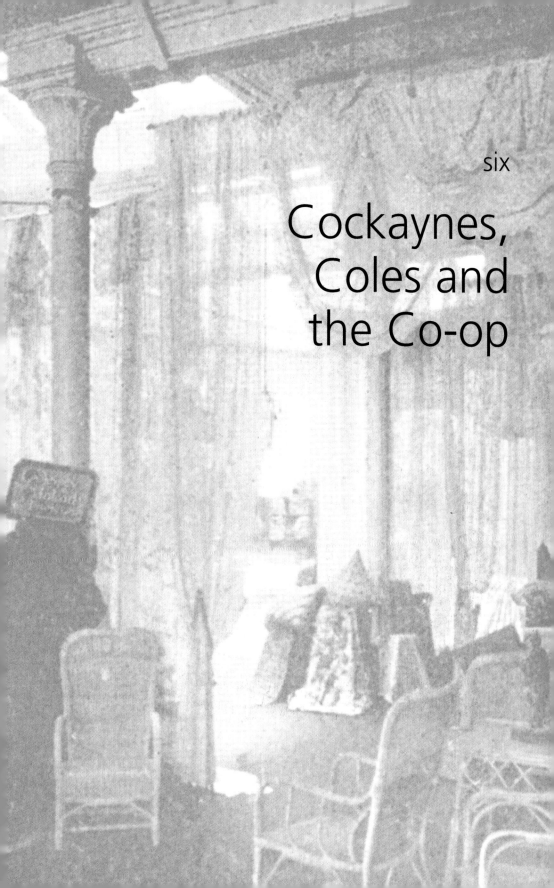

six

Cockaynes,
Coles and
the Co-op

Thomas Bagshawe and William Cockayne set up as drapers in Angel Street, where their father had had a flax dressing business, in 1829. Originally selling linen and woollen drapery, silks, hosiery and ladies' bonnets they were so successful they rebuilt their shop in 1871 and then extended it again in 1876. A further extension in Market Place, seen here around 1900, to the left of the main shop, was added in 1897. Designed by local architects Flockton, Gibbs and Flockton, this took the upper floors across Watson's Walk, which became an elegant 12ft-wide arcade.

A series of views of the interior were taken to mark the store's anniversary in 1919. Almost all shops provided chairs for customers and there was a plentiful supply on the ground floor, where ladies could sit and try on gloves or choose handkerchiefs in comfort. The classic round-seated bentwood chair, seen on the left, was popular in homes as well as shops as it was light and compact but strong. It was designed in 1858 by Thonet Brothers, the famous Austrian furniture manufacturers, and by 1930 fifty million had been produced.

The art needlework and foreign fancy departments. A top-lit light well, creating a galleried interior with some natural light at every level and views of other floors, was now a standard feature of department store design.

The dress fabric department. A huge choice of silk, wool, cotton and linen materials was available for making up into any article of women's or children's clothing. Traditionally the wooden counter tops in drapers' shops had brass rules set into them for measuring out cloth which was sold by the yard (91.5 centimetres) or fractions of a yard.

The new Costume Salon, where large mirrors and comfortable furnishings gave an air of relaxed elegance. High-class stores made clothes to their own designs and would make or alter items for individual customers in their dressmaking departments.

The blouse department from the gallery. A formal white blouse with a tailored suit or skirt was the accepted style of dress for the thousands of women who now worked in offices as clerks or typists. The pipes running across the ceiling look like a water sprinkler system for fighting fires.

The gentlemen's outfitting department. As well as suits and coats this offered everything from collars, ties and socks to outdoor, sporting and travel requisites.

Above: The cabinet furnishing showroom, where furniture of every description was available. From their workshops behind the store Cockaynes could also supply everything necessary to fit, furnish and decorate houses, public buildings, banks and hotels. They had been one of the local firms engaged to supply furniture for Sheffield's new Town Hall in the 1890s.

The soft furnishing department. The tall cast-iron columns and constructional steel beams supporting each floor had different decorative finishes and here provide a tasteful setting for lavish displays of curtain fabrics.

Opposite below: The main staircase and the lift that served all floors. Until American elevators became available in the late nineteenth century, few shops had more than three floors of shopping space as climbing too many stairs was off-putting to customers. Once lifts were installed stores could extend their sales areas onto upper floors previously used for staff offices or living accommodation. Customers were not allowed to operate lifts themselves - this was often the job of a smartly uniformed bellboy.

Opposite above: The restaurant. As well as sales staff in the shop, stores like Cockaynes employed a small army of other staff including waiters, waitresses, cooks and kitchen assistants, providing an extensive menu for three-course lunches and other meals.

Opposite below: The Palm Lounge was available as a less formal venue for teas and light refreshments, often with a musical accompaniment from a pianist or small orchestra.

Above: A page from the 1938 summer sale catalogue. For a long time shops have had sales to clear stock at the end of a season and offer bargains to the shopper. As well as signs in their windows and advertisements in local newspapers Cockaynes produced catalogues of items available.

Right: The sale included furniture at reduced prices. Like Oldham's and other furniture shops Cockaynes offered credit arrangements to customers for larger purchases – £29 10s would be equivalent to over £1,200 today.

Cockaynes was destroyed in 1940, but the business, which had employed over 300 people before the war, carried on in some fifteen different premises. Rebuilding on their Angel Street site began in 1948 with the one storey permitted and in 1953, despite continuing shortages, they put out flags for the Coronation.

Rebuilding the rest of the new shop above the existing ground floor was underway by 1954.

Above: The jewellery and ladies' accessories department in the new store. There are still counters with chairs for customers, but the shop's appearance is one of uncluttered sophistication and goods are displayed very differently compared with the 1919 photographs. The glass cases have interior lighting and the whole floor is evenly lit by fluorescent lights set flush in the ceiling between the nozzles for the fire-extinguishing sprinkler system.

Right: The new shop in 1965, ten years after it was completed. Cockaynes continued in business very successfully after the war and by 1957 had 500 employees.

Left: Cole Brothers was started in 1847 by Thomas, John and Skelton Cole as a family drapery business in Fargate. They were so successful they built this magnificent new shop on the corner of Fargate and Church Street in 1869. It was the first building in Sheffield to rise to six storeys, making the Cutlers' Hall and banks nearby in Church Street seem modest by comparison and setting a standard for commercial architecture in the town that was unrivalled for nearly two decades. Even though the shop was demolished over forty years ago, the corner that was a favourite meeting place for many people is still remembered as 'Coles Corner'.

Below: Coles' private fire brigade in about 1905, apparently in the furnishing department. Large open sales areas full of wooden fittings and valuable but often very flammable stock were at high risk from fire. Major department stores often employed their own firemen until automatic fire detection and water sprinkler extinguishing systems became available.

Fargate in 1900. After it was widened shops were rapidly erected on the new building line in an attractive mixture of Victorian architectural styles and on a scale more in keeping with Coles' original building. The shop now extended further up the street, occupying the two new blocks seen here. The huge plate-glass windows that were such a novelty in Sheffield in 1869 were now commonplace. They gave space for impressive displays of furnishing fabrics like those in the windows on the left.

The haberdashery department in 1934, offering a wide range of items for sewing and mending. The assistant on the right is Miss Hutcheson. Coles became part of Selfridge Provincial Stores before these were bought by the John Lewis Partnership in 1940. Good customer service was an important part of retail success and it was Gordon Selfridge who adopted the slogan, 'the customer is always right', throughout his stores.

The excitement of seeing the new store attracted huge, almost exclusively female, crowds on opening day. For most women a trip to the shops at this date meant wearing a hat and taking a shopping bag – the ladies in the foreground have a nice selection, from a handy string bag to a capacious basket. Most purchases were packaged in paper bags by shop assistants.

Opposite above: Coles' store in Barker's Pool, 1985. After over a century in Fargate, Coles moved to this island site facing the City Hall in 1963. The shop was designed in a crisp, modern style by Yorke, Rosenberg and Mardall, a London firm of architects with a national reputation. It represented a new generation of department stores in the city, with a 400-space multi-storey car park at the rear, linked to each shopping level, to meet the needs of increasingly car-borne shoppers.

Opposite below: Moving out of the Fargate shop in 1963, using wicker baskets and wooden tea chests – the removal man's traditional container.

The perfumery and toiletries department. The clean, streamlined shop fittings and brightly lit displays were a hallmark of the modern department store. The interior, with its painted surfaces and murals, was designed by the Raymond Loewy Corporation of New York, who had recently worked at John Lewis' Oxford Street store in London.

The traditional formality of linen tablecloths, fresh flowers and waitresses with white aprons among the striking modern décor of the restaurant, where tones of green and blue dominated the colour scheme.

The Brightside and Carbrook Co-op's Central Offices and Stores on the corner of Bright Street and Carbrook Street, 1902. The Society was founded in 1868 by a small group of blacksmiths at William Jessop's steelworks with an initial capital of 8s 7d which they used to buy tea and flour. By December that year there were ninety members and they opened their first shop at 39 Carbrook Street. They moved here three years later.

The City Stores, Exchange Street, c. 1929. The B & C went from strength to strength, opening grocery and drapery branches in Wincobank, Grimesthorpe and other suburbs. In 1914, a year after the Sheffield and Ecclesall Co-op opened their city centre shop near The Moor (see page 93), a site on Exchange Street was bought for a new Central Stores. These opened in 1929, in a modern department store rivalling the city's established family drapers.

The shop had a frontage of 200 feet on Exchange Street, and a further 130 feet on Waingate, where the originally single-storey wing was soon extended upwards by two floors. The bronze window frames with integral canopies were set in a surround of dark polished Swedish granite.

The haberdashery counters. Most drapers sold a range of ribbons, lace and other trimmings as well as everything else needed for sewing, knitting and mending. Needlework was part of the school curriculum for girls from 1870 and for many women making and mending clothes for themselves and their families or altering hand-me-downs from friends, employers or charities was a necessity. With materials costing a few pennies, a skilful seamstress could transform an old garment to meet the demands of season, size or fashion.

The millinery department. The interior was designed with fittings of the highest quality in the most up-to-date style, setting it in a class apart from the older Victorian department stores in the city. The doors, doorframes and cabinets like hat drawers were veneered in Ancona walnut with marquetry details such as cross-banded borders and boxwood inlays. The stanchions were encased in Italian marble and the floors were in oak parquetry.

A theatrical display of ladies' fashions. Mannequins with movable hands and arms were now available to give a more life-like appearance to clothes on show than the traditional dressmaker's dummies.

A brilliantly lit display of shoes shows the window-dresser's art of the late 1920s at its most glamorous. The principle of 'less is more' is used to great effect in contrast to the crammed windows of less sophisticated shops. After the introduction of plate glass, the greatest benefit to the art of display was the use of electricity to illuminate windows after dark, offering possibilities undreamt of in the eras of candles and gas lamps. The glass pavement lights provided illumination to basement areas used for storage and packing.

The men and boys' footwear department arranged with regimented formality, relieved only by the patterned Turkey runner on the highly polished floor.

This spectacular array of shirts and ties from the gents' outfitting department seems to have been inspired by the lavish sets of Hollywood musicals that were attracting huge cinema audiences in 1929.

The display in the department itself had a more conventionally sober appearance. Note the selection of trilby hats by the staircase – these were popular wear for well turned-out men in the 1930s and '40s.

The furnishings department with fashionably dark oak furniture and oval mirrors, and an upholstered suite. The three-piece suite, comprising a sofa and two armchairs in matching fabric, was an essential item of furniture for the living room of every ordinary home.

The Lounge Restaurant. The store offered customers a choice of restaurants as well as providing a private dining room for the Society's directors, departmental heads and guests. The main restaurant, on the second floor, was decorated in the Adam style and seated 185 people. The plainer Smokeroom

Restaurant accommodated 100, while the lounge had seating for fifty. Here, amid decorations and furnishings in a charming Oriental style, one could enjoy light refreshments including 'dainty afternoon teas – a restful ending to a busy afternoon's shopping'. These came to an end all too soon, however. From 1939 many customers spent their afternoons engaged in war work and taking tea in canteens, and in 1940 the shop was destroyed by bombs. A new store, Castle House, was eventually completed on a different site, on the corner of Angel Street and Castle Street, and the new Castle Market took over the Exchange Street site.

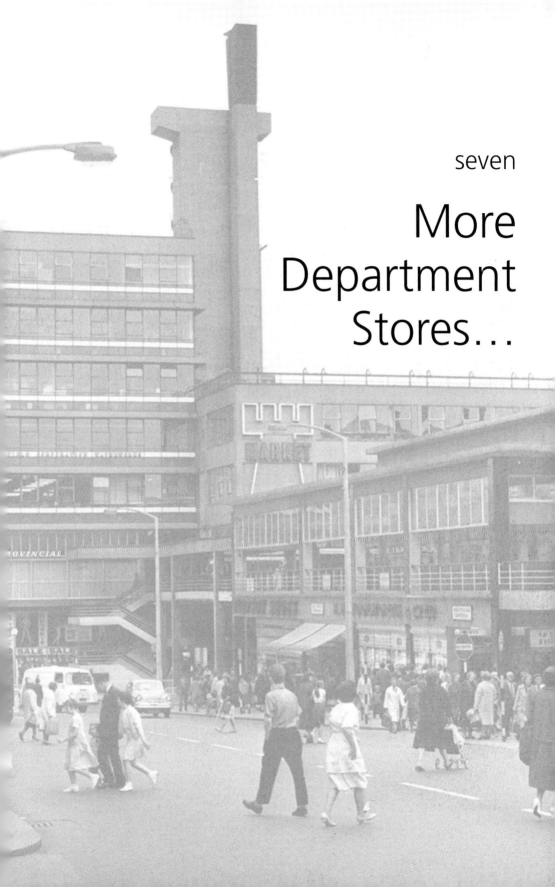

seven

More
Department
Stores…

Above: John Walsh set up his successful business as a ladies' outfitter in High Street in 1875, rapidly expanding the range of goods sold and extending the store into neighbouring properties. By 1895 there were thirty-six departments, selling women's and children's clothing and everything necessary for equipping and furnishing a house. As part of the redevelopment prompted by the widening of High Street a palatial new shop, bringing everything under one roof, was designed by the local architects Flockton and Gibbs and opened in 1899.

Above: Walsh's advertisements were as tasteful and stylish as the customers they were aimed at.

Opposite below: Cabs and private carriages parked beside the crowds thronging the pavement outside Walsh's, *c.* 1900. Large gas lamps hanging from decorative metal brackets in front of the shop were widely used to light window displays. They were less of a fire risk than interior lights and any soot or smoke from an untrimmed wick would not soil the goods.

The burnt-out front of Walsh's after the Blitz. As the main structure had been built with an iron and steel frame to allow an open floor plan, and had fire-resisting floors and staircases, much of the building survived. Although staff were able to salvage the restaurant's silver tea services, cutlery and china from metal cupboards, the days of live music were over.

Like other bombed-out shops, Walsh's resumed trading as soon as possible and they reopened in January 1941 at 'The Mount' at Broomhill. This had been bought in 1914 as a residence for senior female staff, when the staff bedrooms and living accommodation on the top three floors of the shop were taken over for retail use. They also used the Cutlers' Hall for their carpet and furniture galleries and in 1952 were still occupying this shop on the corner of Fargate and Norfolk Row, formerly part of Robert Hanbidge's shop (see page 54).

Walsh's ladieswear department in 1968, when evening gowns were long but daytime hemlines were short. The gaunt ruin of the old shop stood for over ten years until it was finally demolished in 1951. The new shop opened two years later with every luxury a modern department store could offer, its spacious elegance prompting one female reporter to compare it to an ocean liner. Alterations and improvements were completed in 1968 after the adjacent Arundel Gate and Castle Square (Hole-in-the-road) highway scheme was finished.

The menswear department in 1968. Tweed jackets, to be worn with collar and tie, were plentiful, but the polo-neck tops show that the real revolution in men's casual wear had begun.

The sewing room. Traditional services such as altering clothes and making soft furnishings were still carried on behind the scenes in 1968. Walsh's later became Rackham's and was part of House of Fraser stores, but finally closed in 1998, just one year before the shop's centenary on the site.

Opposite above: The restaurant. For many people a city-centre shopping trip was not complete without morning coffee, lunch or afternoon tea and Walsh's continued to provide high-class facilities for leisurely refreshments.

Opposite below: The staff canteen was much more basic, but an important contribution to staff welfare. Improvements to many shop workers' hours and working conditions depended on legislation such as the Early Closing Day and the Offices, Shops and Railway Premises Acts that regulated hours and ensured proper facilities for meal breaks.

Above: C & A Modes store at the bottom of High Street opened in 1932 on the Fitzalan Market site. It was designed by North, Robin and Wilsden in a striking style inspired by Art Deco, American skyscrapers and the work of the Italian Futurists that was quite new to Sheffield. Steel framing supported the upper storeys, allowing them to 'float' above the continuous plate-glass windows of the ground floor.

Opposite above: A tangle of steelwork and part of the front wall was all that remained after three bombs hit the shop in December 1940. Rebuilding started in 1950 and later the store expanded into the former Waring and Gillows building on the corner of Market Place. C & A closed their Sheffield and other UK branches in 2000. The building to the right, facing Fitzalan Square, survived the Blitz and is still in use.

Below: The Sheffield and Ecclesall Co-operative Society's Central Store at the bottom of Cemetery Road, near the junction with Ecclesall Road, was opened in 1913. It was designed by local architect H.L. Patterson and was faced in white 'Marmo' faience. Like its contemporaries, the White Building in Fitzalan Square, the offices of the *Sheffield Telegraph* in High Street, and several of the early cinemas, the building's startling 'self-cleaning' whiteness would have stood out among its soot-blackened neighbours. These later additions along Ecclesall Road were faced in Doulton's faience. The largest block, of 1929, designed by the Co-op's own architect, W.A. Johnson, was decorated with jazzy low-relief patterns and stylised baskets of brightly coloured flowers. Known as The Arcade because of the high internal hall running through the building, it was demolished after closing in 1982, and replaced by a supermarket.

Another drapery business that developed into one of Sheffield's independent department stores was T. and J. Roberts Ltd, founded in 1859 by Thomas Roberts, whose brother John joined him in 1862. They were so successful they built their extensive new store at Moorhead, facing the Crimea Monument, in 1881, and traded there until they closed down in 1937. As so many drapery goods and furnishings displayed in the windows would fade in sunlight, huge fabric awnings, like those seen in other photos, were used to shade them and provide shelter for window-shoppers.

A view up Pinstone Street towards St Paul's church, with Roberts' shop on the left, *c.* 1890. The long front, which extended to the corner of Cambridge Street, had sixty plate-glass windows for displaying goods like the boldly patterned rolls of linoleum. As a practical, hardwearing, inexpensive and easy-to-clean floor covering, lino was widely used for kitchens, halls, corridors, nurseries and servants' bedrooms. Furniture and furnishings were as important as the drapery and clothing side of the business and by 1909 the firm was offering home furnishing packages at £75, £125, £175 and £235, described in their illustrated booklet 'Four Homes'. For £75, a five-roomed house could be completely and comfortably furnished throughout.

The other Roberts' shop, Roberts Brothers Ltd, was on the same side further down The Moor, at Rockingham House, between Rockingham Lane and Rockingham Street. The brothers were John Roberts' two sons, Charles and John Arnold, who set up their own business with four employees in 1896. Like Coles and Cockaynes, Roberts Bros gradually expanded by taking over neighbouring properties, rebuilding in a piecemeal fashion. Their premises, seen here about 1920, extended from No. 32 to No. 54 and included their father's and uncle's original shop at No. 52. Where the pavements were narrower and projecting awnings could have obstructed passing traffic, flat window blinds were often used when the shop was shut, spoiling the fun for window-shoppers and giving the frontage this blank appearance.

The shop was badly damaged in the air raids that devastated The Moor in 1940. The two older blocks, forming the right half of the frontage, were almost completely destroyed.

The newest part of the shop, built in 1937 of steel and concrete, substantially survived. After repairs and a new shop front, trading quickly resumed on the ground floor, although Roberts were prosecuted for spending more than the wartime limit of £500 on building work, and fined £100. Until they rebuilt in the 1950s they also used premises in Ecclesall Road and London Road, and part of T. and J. Roberts' old shop at Moorhead, which they took over in April 1941 (see page 127). In 1952 they were still waiting for rebuilding to start, though plans were in hand. Meanwhile Marks & Spencer's new shop, seen in the distance on the left, was nearing completion.

The Moor in 1963 with the new Rockingham House, and no trams. Due to continuing restrictions on building materials the shop was completed in stages, but Roberts' were able to move into the basement, ground and first floors of the right-hand half in the summer of 1955. The interior followed the latest ideas in shop design, with some goods set out for self-service by customers, a separate cash-till at each sales point and fluorescent lighting. The site for Debenham's store on the right was still empty.

John Atkinson's shop on The Moor in 1905, splendidly decorated for the visit of King Edward VII and Queen Alexandra, who came to open the University of Sheffield. The firm was founded in 1873 and sold household and furnishing drapery as well as 'ribbons, laces, silks, satins, millinery, bonnets, mourning goods, flowers, feathers, Manchester goods, mantles, jackets and shawls'. Today the department store is the only one in the city still run by a family firm and occupying the same site. Marks & Spencer later built their new bazaar on the site of the Methodist New Connexion chapel glimpsed on the right (see page 99).

Atkinson's was damaged beyond repair in December 1940 and the crater left after demolition of the ruins remained until the late 1950s. It was screened from passing shoppers by a temporary window display, seen here in 1950. In January 1941 Atkinson's reopened their business in the Central Picture House on The Moor and the following November took over Johnson and Appleyard's premises, and their stock, on Leopold Street. Atkinson's other temporary shop was on Fargate.

The new shop on The Moor in 1963. Under the policy of complete redevelopment shops and houses that had survived the Blitz were demolished and a new street pattern was set out. Shops of three to five storeys, faced in Portland stone, but in unexciting modern styles, gave the street a completely new character.

Marks & Spencer's first outlet in Sheffield, in the Norfolk Market Hall, 1897. Their method of selling 'small wares' from open counters, so that customers could handle the goods themselves, continued in their shops.

Marks & Spencer's first shop in Sheffield, at 58-60 The Moor, soon after it opened in 1912. The stall in the Norfolk Market Hall carried on for nearly twenty years. As temporary charity or Christmas bazaars sometimes charged an entrance fee and others discouraged casual browsers M & S were at pains to reassure prospective customers that admission was free. They began selling textiles in 1926 and registered their St Michael trademark in 1928.

In 1929 M & S moved a few doors down to a new purpose-built shop, still called a bazaar, at No. 76, on the corner of Eldon Street. The building was left a shattered ruin after the air raids of 1940 and a temporary bazaar operated in the Lansdowne Cinema in London Road until The Moor shop reopened in 1953. A fragment of Atkinson's can be seen beyond on the other corner of Eldon Street (now Holy Green).

The new Marks & Spencer's store under construction in 1952. They had opened their Fargate shop in 1949, so until The Moor shop closed down in August 1990 there were two branches of M & S in the city centre.

The cinema-like front of Woolworth's new store on The Moor in 1953. It was the first permanent shop to be built on The Moor after the war and replaced the bomb-damaged shop that had opened in 1924 as Sheffield's first branch of the American chain. Frank Winfield Woolworth established his 'five and dime' stores in the 1880s and opened his first British 'variety store' in Liverpool in 1909. Like the penny bazaars they displayed goods on open counters so customers could browse.

Haymarket in 1964. Woolworth's had recently moved out of their 1920s shop higher up the street into the block of shops built on the site of the Norfolk Market Hall. Covered bridges at first-floor level linked this to the new Castle Market, which opened in 1960. As the city's main food market it attracted large numbers of shoppers to the area.

Faced in faience like the S. and E. Co-op's Arcade, the great white block of Banner's store at Attercliffe has been a prominent landmark since it opened in 1934. John Banner founded his local drapery and ladies' outfitters business in 1873, when the township was on the brink of a huge population explosion as the great steelworks in the lower Don Valley expanded, drawing thousands of new workers to the area. He moved his shop to the site on Attercliffe Road, at the heart of the thriving shopping centre, in 1894, and rebuilt it on a grand scale, to designs by Sheffield architects Chapman and Jenkinson, four decades later. It was the first shop in the city to have escalators. As the housing round about was demolished in the 1970s, customers dwindled and Banner's closed in 1980.

The proprietor and staff of the Empire Trading Stamp Co. at the entrance of the shop near the top of Howard Street in 1921. The company sold a wide variety of clothing, shoes, household goods, ornaments, luggage and toys. A series of interior photos taken about 1930 provides an unusually complete record of the departments and their displays, though the smartly dressed 'customers' probably aren't real. One can imagine the delight of the lucky assistants let loose in the millinery and coat departments to choose their stylish disguises of cloche hats and fur collars.

The footwear department. Though the styles of most shoes inside have changed, the orderly arrangement of boxes lining the walls is a familiar aspect of the interior of traditional shoe shops today. One can even still find bedroom slippers like those on the display on the left.

The drapery (and umbrella!) department, where customers, apparently accompanied by their dog, could sit on bentwood chairs while deferential shop assistants in suitably unbecoming overalls laid out goods on the counter for inspection.

The china and ornament department showed a fine display of figurines below a shelf of elaborately decorated bedroom sets of washing bowl, chamber pot and water jug. On the top shelf the three-part sets of a pair of vases and a bowl were designed to grace the top of a china cabinet, sideboard or mantelpiece. Note the fashion for wearing ankle socks with high heels! The uncanny similarity between the shop assistant on the right and the formidable customer brandishing her shopping list in the previous photo, not to mention the unusual incidence of identical twins working as shop assistants in different departments, confirms the suspicion that these photos were all staged. Note, too, the same black dog attached to different 'customers' and sitting here in unrepentant disregard of the 'dogs not admitted' sign.

The other half of the china department made good use of every inch of display space available with squadrons of jugs suspended from the ceiling and flying across the wall, and tableware piled on shelves beneath the small display stand. It is not surprising that dogs were not welcome!

Behind the main shop building, glass-roofed extensions provided further display space for the extensive range of goods stocked. Here more fancy china crowds the shelves with a bewildering array of vases, cake stands and dishes in plain, cut and coloured glass. On the top shelf are oil lamps with their big glass mantles that required a delicate touch to clean and were easily broken. A pile of large sheets of brown wrapping paper and roll of string appear on the counter in several of the photos – purchases would be neatly wrapped and tied to be carried home. Today's ubiquitous plastic carrier bag was a long way in the future.

Workaday enamelled pans sitting among a fine array of polished brass and copper fenders and fire screens, and the big copper kettles that were kept in constant use on the fire or range to provide a supply of hot water in many homes. The basketwork coal containers doubled as a handy fireside seat.

More enamel kitchenware, including bread and big cylindrical flour bins, colanders, jugs and saucepans. Enamelware was popular in the 1920s and '30s as it is durable, hygienic and easy to clean, and came in a range of dark and pastel colours, introducing a more attractive note to kitchenware, which was traditionally made of wood or iron. The cabinets on the rear wall are meat safes, for safe storage of raw and cooked meats, dairy products and other perishable foods in a larder or cellar, when very few homes had a refrigerator. Their fine wire-mesh panels allowed air to circulate to keep food cool but kept flies and other insects off it. The three large oval domed mesh covers hanging with them would fit over the traditional china dish on which the Sunday joint was served.

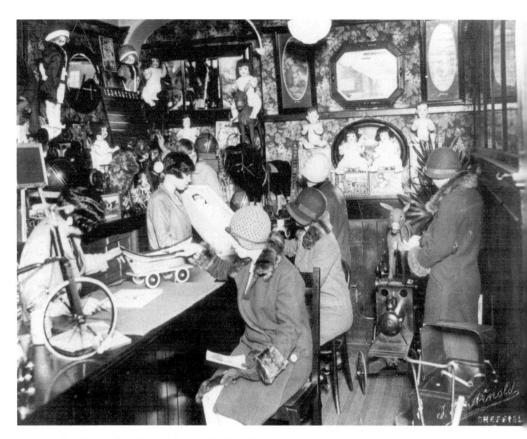

The toy department doesn't seem very child-friendly by today's standards – almost all the toys are high up and out of reach and the dark wood fittings and sombre wallpaper are rather gloomy. These more expensive toys are much more likely to have been bought by adults as presents for children than selected by children themselves. The simple pleasures offered by a wheeled boat or railway engine have now been replaced by battery-powered equivalents, but dolls and bicycles are always popular.

eight

Speciality
Shopping

Above: Harris Leon Brown's jewellers shop, Market Place, *c.* 1925. Brown was a Jewish immigrant from Poland who fled to England. He established his business here in 1861 and built up a reputation as one of Sheffield's principal jewellers, gold and silversmiths, watchmakers and diamond merchants. The prominent coat of arms is the Duke of Norfolk's – Brown was appointed as jeweller to the 15th duke and the shop, now in Barker's Pool, has continued to serve his successors.

Opposite above: The magnificent showrooms where Sheffield's silverware and cutlery manufacturers displayed their goods have long gone. This spacious carpeted room with its elaborate plaster ceiling and brilliant displays of goods laid out in glass-topped mahogany cases belonged to Joseph Rodgers and Sons Ltd. They first opened their showroom in Norfolk Street in 1821 – this photo was taken in the late nineteenth century after it had been made even more luxurious.

Below: Beal's jewellery shop in the Fitzalan Market, on the corner of King Street and Market Place, *c.* 1920. Michael Beal trained as a watchmaker and jeweller in the 1820s and eventually established his business here in around 1860. A Chartist in his youth, he supported his friend Ebenezer Elliott in the campaign against the Corn Laws and was a Liberal councillor and then Alderman on the town council from 1853 to 1883. As founder of the Chamber of Industry and Board of Arbitration he helped to resolve local strikes and lockouts.

Joseph William Thornton opened his first confectionery shop in 1911 on this corner of Howard Street and Norfolk Street. By 1970 it was part of a nationwide chain of over a hundred Chocolate Kabins. Their distinctive lettering and enticing offer of 'Bon-Bons' gave the shops an air of indulgent luxury. This shop was demolished to make way for the new Town Hall extension.

Thornton's second shop was on The Moor, where the family lived over the shop and made boiled sweets, such as fish mixtures and mint rock, in the cellar. The company's first chocolates were violet creams, made on the ground floor where pieces of fondant flavoured with Otto of Violets were dipped in chocolate by hand and decorated with sugared violet petals. Thornton's famous Special Toffee was introduced in 1925. The Moor shop was lost in the Blitz and in 1956 Thornton's still occupied this temporary shop at the beginning of London Road. Fortunately sugar, cream and other ingredients for their 'freshly made' chocolates were no longer rationed.

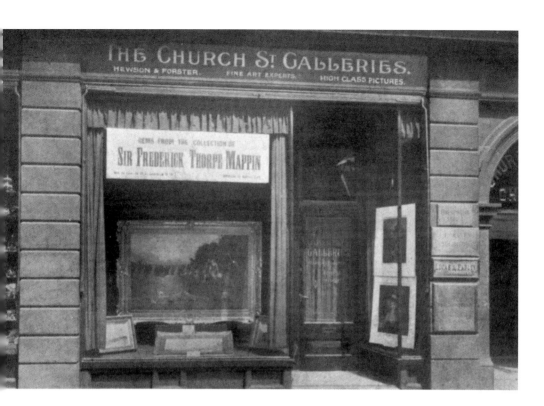

Above: The Church Street Galleries in 1914. They were opened a few years earlier by two of the city's leading fine-art dealers, William Hewson and Robert John Forster. Sir Frederick Thorpe Mappin was the nephew of John Newton Mappin, who founded the Mappin Art Gallery, and, like him, was a great art collector. During his lifetime he gave over eighty paintings to the gallery, but after his death in 1910 many of the remaining pictures in his collection were sold.

Right: Robert William Watson moved his business from Angel Street (hence The Angel Pharmacy) to 84 High Street, seen here, in about 1900. James Reginald Norris joined as his new partner and they provided a special showroom for photographic equipment. Kodak's Box Brownie camera – which was cheap, simple and easy to operate – was introduced in 1900, enabling many more people to take up photography as a hobby.

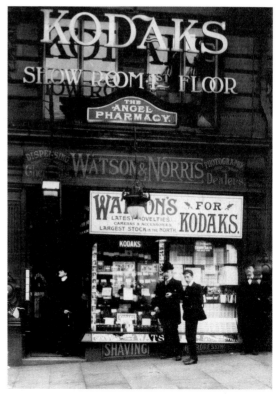

Above: Market Place and the Fitzalan Market, looking towards Angel Street, in about 1890. The post office had occupied the central portion of the building, now Colver's outfitters, from 1850 to 1871. Thomas Cook started his tourism business in Leicester in 1841 when he organised a rail excursion to a temperance rally for 500 people. Their Sheffield 'excursionist's office' moved here from Change Alley nearby in 1888 and by 1893 the firm was advertised as 'tourist, excursion, emigration and shipping agents'. Cook's reasonably priced package tours made foreign holidays affordable by the growing middle classes for the first time.

Left: The top of end of the Fitzalan Market Hall, facing Market Place, *c.* 1885. Thomas Rodgers, who ran a business as a printer, lithographer and engraver, stationer and bookseller occupied the shop at this corner for over thirty years.

Charles Atkinson's newsagents in Pond Hill displaying placards and posters with the day's national, international and sporting news on 20 April 1899. By the late nineteenth century developments in printing techniques allowed magazines to include a wide variety of illustrations and there was an explosion in the range of cheap printed reading matter to meet the needs of an increasingly literate population. Most adults, however poor, would have had the benefit of education in the Board schools introduced by the Elementary Education Act of 1870, which made attendance at school between the ages of five and thirteen compulsory. The city's two daily papers catered for a cross section of political views, *The Independent* taking a Liberal stance and *The Telegraph* supporting the Conservatives. Both covered the whole range of current news available and it could now be received almost immediately. As a result of Marconi's work on radio waves Britain was linked with Europe by wireless telegraphy in the year this photo was taken, while news from the United States still came via marine telegraph cables, first laid successfully across the Atlantic in 1866.

George Arthur Fox at his shop on Ecclesall Road, *c.* 1908. He was born in 1872 and started his working life as a grocer's assistant but took over his parents' newsagents business at No. 128 after they died in the 1890s. He moved two doors along to No. 130 around 1904. He later took up conjuring under the stage name of Professor De Lyle and by 1910 had given up the shop, continuing to work as a professional conjuror until he was well over seventy.

Mrs Martha Alice Baylis' tobacconists shop is listed at 585 Queen's Road in the 1906 and 1910 local directories. The wide range of cigarettes and loose tobacco she stocked is only available in specialist shops now. Theatres often printed small bills for newsagents and tobacconists to display as well as the large bills pasted on walls (see page 50).

Above: Only a few steps from Fargate, in 1915 Norfolk Street was home to a variety of small shops such as E.F. Jones' tobacconists, Walter F. Bown's jewellers and Henry Outram's sweetshop. The tradition of selling snuff at No. 87 was passed on to Hays, though the building was later re-fronted with mock half-timbering.

Right: Hays' tobacconists shop at 87 Norfolk Street was one of the best-known outlets for Sheffield snuff. The Wilson family started making snuff at Sharrow in 1737, using a water-powered mill to grind tobacco into the fine powder or 'flour' after the leaves had been matured and turned and a secret recipe of oils and essences added. Following a split in the family Joseph and Henry Wilson set up a rival operation at the adjoining Westbrook Mill in 1833. This photo was taken in 1934, the year after their firm celebrated its centenary. The figure of the kilted highlander was part of their advertising. The flags are probably flying for the royal visit of the Duchess of York (later the Queen Mother) who came to open the new Central Library and Graves Art Gallery nearby in Surrey Street on 5 July.

Above: Wilson Peck's original premises, on the corner of Pinstone Street and what is now Barker's Pool (then Fargate), *c.* 1900. The Albert Hall can be seen in the background. The firm of Arthur Wilson, Peck and Co. Ltd, established in 1892, was a much-loved Sheffield institution supplying the wants of the city's professional and amateur musicians and music lovers for over a century. On the floors above this shop they also provided teaching rooms for over twenty music professors. Arthur Wilson was the pseudonym of Henry Mushet, who preferred music to his distinguished metallurgical family's steel business. In 1883 he was trading as the German Piano Agency in West Street, while John Peck, his future partner, was selling music and musical instruments in Church Street. Peck was a talented violinist and music teacher who performed at Sheffield's Albert Hall as leader of orchestras conducted by Elgar, Charles Hallé and Henry Wood.

Opposite above: In about 1904 they moved to the shop on the opposite corner, formerly occupied by the cabinetmakers, Johnson and Appleyard's (who, in a sort of retail musical chairs, moved into a new shop seen on the right in the photos). They advertised themselves as 'pianoforte, harmonium and American organ merchants, tuners & repairers, sole agents for the Bechstein pianos...pianists and quadrille bands supplied...', although their association with the German piano firm was severed during the First World War. Changes in musical tastes and home entertainment, and especially competition from television, led to a decline in the piano trade from the 1960s and Wilson Peck was forced to move out of Beethoven House to smaller premises in 1988, finally closing altogether in 2001.

Right: Three self-possessed sales assistants in front of Wilkinson's stationery stall in the Norfolk Market Hall, *c.* 1906. They also sold books and a wide range of postcards and were one of the earliest, if not the first, outlet for both Edison's phonographs and gramophone records in Sheffield. Two-sided records had recently been introduced – the 10- or 12-inch discs had playing times of about three or four and a half minutes on each side and they soon overtook the older cylindrical phonograph recordings in popularity.

Horses were still the main source of power for private and commercial transport when Samuel Pottinger transferred his saddlery business to Division Street about 1905. The large range of equipment and accessories he made included the halters, bridles and harnesses seen here, c. 1910. He is standing on the left with his younger brother, Jabez, on the right. The business closed down after Samuel died in 1922.

William Greaves' cycle shop on Middlewood Road, Hillsborough, c. 1905. Cycling clubs had been started in Sheffield in the 1880s organising both outings and races for members and cycling was popular with both sexes. While mass-produced models were available from companies such as Raleigh in Nottingham, good local shops like this could also make custom-built bicycles from components supplied by a variety of manufacturers.

The glamorous owner of a smart new model outside Wragg's car, motorcycle and bicycle showroom on Leopold Street, *c*. 1925. Sheffield's own car manufacturing industry survived until the early 1920s but could not compete with the mass-produced models available from the assembly lines of Austin and Morris. The price of Austin's 'Seven' fell from £225 when introduced in 1922, to £125 in 1928, bringing it within the reach of the middle classes.

Bicycles and motorbikes from BSA (Birmingham Small Arms), one of the leading British makers, in the showroom. Walter Wragg was a pioneer of the cycle and motor trade in Sheffield. In 1892, when he was only eighteen, he set up as a cycle maker and agent in Attercliffe and built machines for several prominent racing cyclists. He later built a tri-car with a water-cooled engine and was the owner of three De Dion single-cylinder motor cars. He opened his shop on Pinstone Street in 1907.

The offices and showroom of Renton, Holdsworth and Co., colliery engineers, in Norfolk Street, c. 1925. The coal mines in Sheffield and south Yorkshire depended on the services of such professionals but it seems unlikely that this display of equipment for servicing and ventilating them would have attracted much passing trade!

Edward Brewitt and his wife Betsy at their shop in Asline Road, Heeley, c. 1895. Gas, rather than electric lighting would have been standard in new homes at this date and a huge range of decorative fittings was available. As bathrooms and fixed hot-water plumbing became more common the need for hot-water tanks increased. The skills needed to work with lead pipes for gas and water were equally useful for bell hanging.

nine

Delivery,
Mail Order
and Other
Conveniences

A Coles' van in an immaculately swept Rustlings Road, *c.* 1900. Delivering customers' purchases was once part of the service of most shops, whether it was by means of the traditional 'butcher's boy' on a bicycle with a large basket at the front or with a fleet of vans.

Delivery vans also came in useful in emergencies – here Coles partners queue up to be taken home during the bus strike in Sheffield in October 1955. When Coles became part of the John Lewis Partnership in 1940 it joined a group of shops that involved all staff in the business in a unique way. The partnership system was introduced by John Lewis' son, Spedan Lewis, after he took over the management of their Peter Jones shop in London in 1914. Everyone working for the partnership, whether a shop assistant or manager, had a share in the business and benefited from the profits. Working terms and conditions were also better than in most of the retail sector, which was notorious for long hours and low wages.

Cockaynes' delivery vans outside the shop in Angel Street, *c.* 1920.

The staff of Cockaynes transport department on Psalter Lane, *c.* 1920. From left to right, back row includes: Harold Thomas, Frank Gouldsborough, Howard Pratt, William Turner, H.S. Ringwood, Sam Green, and Horace Hutton. Middle row: Harvey Bell, –?– , Freddie Pratt, Herbert Beighton, Reg Marsh, –?–. Front row: John Smith, Johnny Townsend, ? Tibenham.

The Sheffield philanthropist J.G. Graves made his fortune through his pioneering mail-order business. Originally selling watches by post he expanded the range of goods in response to demand and sent them all over the world. This photograph was taken about 1900 when his head office occupied the old water company building in Division Street.

In 1903 Graves moved his business to a huge new building, 'Westville' on Durham Road. In the offices and storerooms an army of clerks and packers carried out the vast operation of dealing with orders and dispatching goods. At the height of his success Graves employed 3,000 people in Sheffield. Most of the staff in the offices were women, some seen here, *c.* 1925.

The dispatch department about 1925, with blankets and bedding ready for wrapping. Mail order was a godsend for people like emigrants to Australia and Canada who could buy familiar goods that weren't available in their new, sometimes very remote, homes, even though they might have to wait many weeks for them to arrive.

The dispatch and packing section of the footwear department, *c.* 1925. Customers selected the goods they ordered from illustrated catalogues and Graves set up his own printing department to produce these.

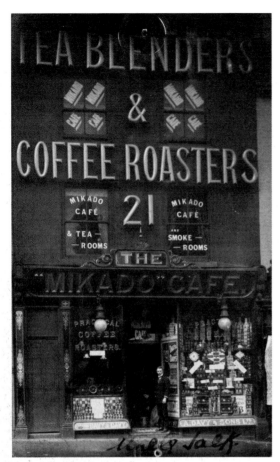

Left: Davy's Mikado Café on Haymarket, *c.* 1910. Shopping as a leisure activity is not a new phenomenon and cafés like Davy's offered a welcome opportunity to rest and review one's purchases or compare notes with friends.

Below: Barker's Pool, looking towards Division Street, *c.* 1890. The small building on the left is the urinal installed in 1876. These welcome 'temples of convenience' caused great controversy when they were first introduced, as no shopkeeper wanted them sited near their shop. Sheffield's women had to wait until 1896 for similar relief, when the underground public conveniences at the new Town Hall were opened. A report to the Health Committee observed that as they were used on 11,521 occasions in the first year, they were obviously much appreciated.

Moorhead in 1952, with the base of the Crimea Monument and Roberts Bros temporary shop in part of T. and J. Roberts' former premises. The monument was the focal point of The Moor shopping area from 1862 until it was removed in 1957. It was the traditional site of a cab rank and ice-cream seller and provided a drinking fountain, public conveniences, and a transport information kiosk – all helping to make a shopping trip more enjoyable and get one home safely at the end of the day.

Other local titles published by Tempus

Haunted Sheffield
MR AND MRS P. DREADFUL

This work presents a chilling collection of stories of apparitions, manifestations, strange sightings and happenings in the streets, churches and buildings of Sheffield. Compiled by the notorious ghost-hunting couple, Mr and Mrs P. Dreadful, this book is essential reading for anyone interested in the paranormal history of the city.

978 07524 4195 5

Sheffield Parks and Gardens
DOUG HINDMARCH

Sheffield is justifiably proud of the parks, woodland and open spaces which make it one of the greenest cities in Europe. However, in the early nineteenth century, there were few green spaces in this crowded, polluted industrial town. This book illustrates how the people of the city acquired and developed their beautiful parks and gardens from the 1830s onwards, with rare images of long-disappeared park features.

978 07524 3542 8

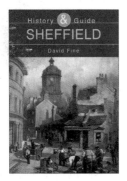

Sheffield History & Guide
DAVID FINE

This highly readable account of Sheffield's past considers the impact of the vast steel-rolling mills, compares the lives of mill owner and mill worker, and looks at life in the countless back-to-backs once strewn across this richly varied city. Using a wealth of photographs, maps and prints, David Fine brings the story up to date and considers what the future may hold for Sheffield.

978 07524 2953 3

Sheffield Cinemas
CLIFFORD SHAW

Through the medium of old photographs, programmes and advertisements, this book provides a fascinating look at the history of cinema-going in Sheffield over the last century. Including insights into the technology behind the silver screen, the entrepreneurs and the cinema chains who operated in the city, as well as the stars, staff and spectators, *Sheffield Cinemas* reveals how the experience of seeing a film at the cinema has changed over the decades.

978 07524 2293 0

If you are interested in purchasing other books published by Tempus, or in case you have difficulty finding any Tempus books in your local bookshop, you can also place orders directly through our website

www.tempus-publishing.com